THE ULTIMATE REFERR

PROFESSIONALS

The Machine To Magnetically Attract All The Referrals You'll Ever Need So You'll Never Have To Cold Call Again!!!

Author and Business Coach
DAVID L. SIMS

DEDICATION

I dedicate this book to the memory of Dr. Donald W.
Kreutzer (March 8, 1938 - February 1, 2015). He was a
captain in the Green Beret, a Viet Nam veteran, a
pathologist. He was my mentor, my father figure, my
friend, and my leader. Most of all he showed me that
there was more than "smoke-drink-roll" in life. He
taught me discipline, ethics, principles, and life long
learning. But most of all he taught me that people "vote
with their feet."

CONTENTS

CONTENTS (continued)

FORWARD
WHY DO 80% TO 90% OF PEOPLE WHO START A BUSINESS FAIL WITHIN THE FIRST 4 TO 5 YEARS?

It's a startling fact that 80% to 90% of businesses started by people who've never run a business before go broke in just a short time. Why? There are many reasons but the three major ones are as follows: **One**, people really don't understand marketing or how to market their business. **Two,** people don't know how to sell. For some reason many people in business think that selling is evil. They think of the used car salesman with the plaid coat and the high pressure pitch. They don't understand that selling is critical for growth.

However, usually nothing happens in a business until a sales is made. I don't care if you own an architectural firm, an accounting firm, a law firm, a dental practice, etc.

Third, the third reason business owners go broke is that they have the wrong systems in place for running their business. In this book you'll learn a system that will help you in all three of these arenas.

When I began my business 30 years ago I began by cold-calling. The reason, I didn't know anything else to do plus the people advising me suggested that I do that. I worked hard every work day of the week. I was getting desperate and depressed because I couldn't make a sale. I had creditors calling me saying, "You promised you'd send us money. Where is it?" I barely had enough money to put gas in my car. I was waking up in the middle of the night with a knot in my stomach worrying if I was going to succeed or not.

I made 150 cold-call sales presentations in a two and one-half month period before I made my first sale for $250. Out of that sale of $250 I had to take $150 to buy the inventory. So I ended up with a $100.00 gross profit. I don't care how frugal and thrifty you are, it's hard to make it grossing only $100.00 every two and one-half months.

The next week I received a referral to a decision-maker by someone who had **influence** with that decision-maker. The person referring me suggested that I meet with the prospect. He gave me his name, his telephone number, and why he needed my help. That was the first referral I'd ever received. I made the call to schedule the appointment. I got right through. There was no resistance to set the appointment. The next week I showed up and there was no resistance in the sales presentation. 45 minutes later I walked out with an order for $2,500.00 and a check for $1,250.00.

That's when I began my quest and search for more information about Referrals. I found very little so I began gathering and acquiring information from as many top producers as I could find. A lot of the information you'll find in this book came from producers who earned either a 6 figure income or a 7 figure income. They were very guarded with their referral strategies they used to generate their fortunes. They didn't want to share them with coworkers, other people in their field or other professionals.

I was fortunate to gain their trust and piece this system together bit-by-bit. The results from using this system are that I've had people who'd never sold anything before being able to make millions of dollars in sales in their first year. You may not make those kinds of sales but if you follow the strategies in this book your sales will surely grow and it won't take long.

Now let's get started.

David L. Sims
Founder and CEO of The David Sims Coaching Company
david@davidsimscoaching.com
417-831-0050

CHAPTER 1

WHY REFERRALS ARE CRITICAL FOR YOU TO GROW YOUR BUSINESS AND INCOME!!!

Hello. This is David Sims. I've put this system together for you for one purpose only. That purpose is to put more money into your pocketbook. Would you be O.K. with that? The way we are going to do this is to help you understand and implement the system we've developed. This system's development has taken years to refine and fine-tune.

First I want to commend you for participating in this system. We live in a country and time where there is more growth and opportunity than ever before. Sadly, studies show us that less than 10% of the people in our country truly take advantage of this opportunity.

I know you are in the 10% group because you are participating in this system and you will become more successful as a result.

Systems Are Critical
For Running Your Business

One of the best ways to take advantage of the opportunity that's available to you is to have a Proven System. Several years ago the largest computer company in the industry was IBM. You probably recognize the name. One of the reasons they attributed to their success was summed up in their slogan. Their slogan was, "The System Is The Solution." They definitely felt that a good system was important.

The E-Myth: Why Systems Are Critical For Your Business Growth

Some years later an excellent book was written about the importance of systems. The title was, **"The E-Myth"**. And the author was Michael Gerber. Michael does a great job of describing the necessity of having a great system to run your business.

Everyone in business needs a Proven system. It doesn't matter if you are the president of a company with 1000 employees or if you are in business by yourself.

The better the systems you have in place to run your business the more successful you will be. Think about one of the most successful franchises of today. That franchise is McDonald's. McDonald's have such excellent systems in place that million dollar businesses are run by people from all walks of life.

You will possibly see a million dollar business run mostly by high-school juniors and seniors. There are several other examples of large businesses that have great systems in place. What you will see is this, the more successful the business, the better the systems they have in place for managing and operations.

Total Quality Management-
What Role Does It Play?

How about Dr. Edwards Deming?   He was one of the creators of the concept of "Total Quality Management". *TQM* Total Quality Management was a business philosophy adopted by the country of Japan after World War Two.

Dr. Deming met with the industrial leaders of Japan and informed them that if they wanted to be a super power in business they would have to create excellent systems in their manufacturing plants and they would have to focus on quality. That is exactly what they did.

 Now you will find everything from watches to automobiles being manufactured in Japan. These products are usually the ones most often sought after by consumers.

One of the significant statements Dr. Deming made during one of his speeches was this, ***"94% of all problems in a company come from the systems in place. Only 6% of the problems come from people."*** Think about it, most business owners think the reason they struggle in business is they can't find good help.

What Dr. Deming is saying is the reason they are struggling is because of their systems that have evolved as the company has evolved. Everyone in business has a set of systems in place for operations. You may not realize this but you're running your business with a set of systems you've developed over the years.

Some systems are more effective than others. You have systems for sales, marketing, customer service, and managing your company. *"If you are not making the progress you'd like to make and think you are capable of making, it could be because of the systems you have in place."* This is why I've put together this Referral system for you. If you want to enjoy more success all you have to do is to follow this system and implement it.

CHAPTER 2
HOW DOES THE SLIGHT EDGE HELP YOU GROW YOUR BUSINESS?

Another important concept for you to understand is the concept of *"The Slight Edge"*. The "Slight Edge" concept means you don't have to make great advances to enjoy success. The concept says you don't have to <u>be 10 times as good as you are right now to enjoy 10 times the results</u>. The concept says you just have to be a little better in a "few key areas" to generate greater success. Do you know anyone who earns 10 times the amount of money you earn?

 If you do, are they ten times as smart as you? Do they work ten times as hard? Are they ten times better looking than you? I would bet you answered "NO" to all three of those questions. The people you know who are more successful are just doing a few of the right things a little better than you are. You are now beginning the system that will give you the slight edge in business.

Slight Edge Examples

Let me give you a couple of instances where "the slight edge" makes a big difference in results. Several years ago Pat Riley was the coach of the professional basketball team, the Los Angeles Lakers. One year the team won the NBA title and was crowned world champions. The following year they were eliminated in the first round of the playoffs.

This happened to essentially the same team that had just 12 months prior beaten everyone to win the championship. So the following year Coach Riley implemented "**The Slight Edge**" concept with his team. He told each of his players to pick out 5-key areas of their game. It could be rebounding, free throw shooting, or field goal percentage, etc.

It could be any of the critical areas of their game. He told them he wanted them to focus on each of these 5 areas and their goal was to improve **only one percent** over last year's numbers. He just wanted them to improve one percent from the previous year.

Now let me ask you a very simple question. Can you improve just one percent over last year? Could you pick out five areas of your key activities and improve one percent over your previous years production?

Here was the reasoning behind Coach Riley's thinking. He had 12 players on the team. He reasoned that if each player were to improve one percent in five different categories that would mean a five percent increase for that person. If each of the 12 players improved five percent that would mean a 60% increase for the team.

But here's what really happened to the team. (Also, this could happen for you.) As each player focused on their five areas and measured their monthly progress Coach Riley found not only a one percent increase in production in each area but some had 20%, 25%, and even 100% increases in their production. **That next year the team went on to win another NBA championship.**

Let me give you another sample of the **slight edge** in action. This is another sports example. You can find several examples in the different sports. The reason these examples are easy to find in sports is that the different sports professions do such an outstanding job of measuring activity and results. (There's a good message for you in that last statement.)

But a good example to use is the sport of baseball. Let's compare two batters and see how "**the slight edge**" may impact their results. We will name the two batters A and B. Imagine batter A is at bat ten times. During those ten at bats he gets two hits. His batting average is then .200.

What is the salary of a hitter in professional baseball with a batting average of .200? At this time the salary may be two hundred to five hundred thousand dollars. Now batter B gets up to bat ten times. During those ten at bats he gets three hits. What's the batting average for batter B? His batting average is .300. What is the yearly income of a .300 hitter in professional baseball? His income is probably 3 to 5 million dollars a year, or maybe more.

Batter B is going to have an income of about ten times batter A. But what is their difference in production? The difference is that **batter "B" had one more hit in ten at bats then batter "A".** Batter B didn't have ten times the number of hits; he just had one more hit in ten at bats but look at the results he produced. That's the point I want to drive home to you. The point is that you don't have to have ten times the production you have now to greatly increase your results.

So our goal is to get you to focus on a few key areas. Can you see how growing your production doesn't have to be as hard as you thought it would?

Chapter 3
What Do You Need To Succeed In Business?

When you are growing your business there are four critical areas you need to excel in to build a prosperous business. These four areas are "Sales, Marketing, Customer Service, and Organization." These are all important. A good visual to use is a chair with four legs. Each of the four areas represents a leg on your chair of your success.

What would happen if you removed one of the legs? Don't you think that it would be very hard to get the chair to sit upright without falling over? You could probably balance the chair as you tried to set in it. But it would take a lot of work and would be very uncomfortable.

This is comparable to your business. I don't know if one area is more important than another. Maybe you will think that sales and marketing are more important than your organizational skills.

However, I've known companies to have tremendous growth. Their growth was so great that they went out of business because they couldn't manage it. So maybe you'll see that all areas are important for you as you are growing your business.

Your question may be, "<u>what do these four areas have to do with the system I'm going to learn to implement?</u>" That's a great question. Each of these areas will be impacted by the system you will be implementing. The first area to discuss is that of sales. How do you think this referral system is going to affect you and your sales process?

How Will The Referral System Affect Your Sales?

Many years ago I met a gentleman I considered to be an excellent salesman. I asked him what he thought to be the most important part of the sales process. His reply was that his idea of the most important part of the sales process was "prospecting". I found this hard to believe so I asked him to explain.

He replied with this statement. He said, *"I would rather be a master prospector than a wizard of speech with no one to tell my story to."*   He went on to say that he didn't feel like he was a very good salesman but that he was a great prospector.

He said, "**if I have a really good prospect then I don't have to be a very good salesman.**" That concept took me some time to comprehend but once   I got it, it made all the difference in my business growth. I even went so far as to develop a measuring system to measure the quality of my prospects. So what does this mean for you? Does the quality of your prospect really affect the sales process for you?

Why Is Referral Prospecting
So Important For Your Ability To Sell?

Let me give you a formula about the sales system to see if it makes sense to you. The formula is this. "take a prospect and put the prospect together with a salesperson and if everything goes right you will end up with a sale." Does that make sense? So the formula simply stated is this, "prospect plus salesperson equals a sale." That's a rather simple formula, isn't it?

Now what I want you to do is to make it a little more sophisticated so you can understand the value of prospecting. I want you to assign a number between one and ten to your prospect. The better the prospect for you the higher the number you assign to them.

You may ask, "how can I tell the quality of my prospect?" You'll have three kinds of prospects. Class A; class B; and class C prospects. The old stand-by definition of a class A prospect has three parts. First, does the prospect have a need for your product or service? Second, does the prospect have the money needed to purchase or are they willing to purchase what you are selling? And third, does the prospect have the ability to make a decision to purchase what you are selling?

So the old definition of a Class A prospect was simply someone having the need, the money, and the ability to make a decision. But what if you added a fourth characteristic to this definition.

What if you were introduced to this prospect by someone having influence with them and during that introduction there was a strong recommendation that the prospect grant you an appointment to see you and hear what you have to say?

Would that increase the value of that prospect for you? On a scale of one to ten with ten being the highest rating a prospect could get, you would probably have a excellently qualified prospect. That number would probably be a 7, 8, 9, or 10.

Now what do you think about rating the salesperson? What if you were to rate a salesperson on a scale of one to ten? With the number "one" on the scale representing a rookie in the field of sales with very little experience, technical knowledge, limited sales skills, and very little polish.

On the other end of the scale is a salesperson ranking towards the number "ten". This number represents someone having experience, polish, technical knowledge, and great experience in the field of selling. What you will find is that every prospect and every salesperson falls somewhere between the number one and the number ten.

Now let's take this concept one step farther. We will assign a number to the prospect and a number to the salesperson. Those two numbers must add up to the number "ten" to achieve a sale.

So as you learned previously the formula would go like this, "prospect plus sales person equals a sale." To make the formula work we must assign a number to the prospect, and then assign a number to the salesperson, and those two numbers must combine to equal at least ten. And the number "ten" signifies you've made a sale.

What if you were to assign the number "5" to a class "A" prospect? That means that the salesperson must be at least a "5" on the sales chart for the two numbers to add up to the number "ten," thus meaning a sale. If a class "A" prospect is a 5 on the chart then what about a class "B" prospect? Would this prospect be a "4" or a "3"? What about a class "C" prospect are they a "3" or a "2"?

You may be asking what are these other two prospects. A class "B" prospect has only two of the three criteria that a class "A" prospect may possess. A class "B" prospect may only have the need and ability to make a decision but they may not have any money and they may not be willing to try to get the money. A class "C" prospect will have only one of the three qualities of a class "A" prospect.

So if you were calling on a class "C" prospect and they only registered a "2" on your prospect scale then you would have to be an "8" on the sales side to be able to combine the two numbers to generate a sale.

Most often when you are cold calling, the prospects you find will be the "2's" and "3's". You may occasionally find one qualifying higher on the scale but they are so few and far between that it's tough to build a client base with this method. So do you see why it is so difficult to sell cold calling?

CHAPTER 4

THE BETTER THE PROSPECT,
THE EASIER THE SELLING BECOMES!

Now do you understand this concept? <u>Do you see why prospecting is the most important aspect of selling?</u> If all of your prospects were "7's" and "8's" wouldn't it be easier for you to sell? If all of your prospects were "7's" or "8's" you would only have to be a "2" or "3" or the sales side to complete the sale.

It will be very difficult for you to achieve this quality of prospects by direct marketing methods. So that brings up another question, "<u>why is it so difficult in these days and times to acquire good prospects by direct marketing systems?</u>"

There's A Lot Of NOISE In The Market Place.

The answer is "Noise". Are you familiar with the term marketing "Noise?" "Noise" is the sound you hear when the radio station you are listening to temporarily goes off the air. If the station doesn't come back on in a short time you either ignore the sound or change channels.

Now what is "Noise" when it comes to advertising? You are now exposed to so much advertising you will have a tendency to shut it out. You are constantly being bombarded with ads. There are several factors contributing to this. First, you see "ten-times" as many ads now in a 24-hour period than you did ten years ago in a "two-week" period.

It wasn't that many years ago when there were more personal computers sold in the U.S. than were televisions. Over half of the people in the U.S. have now purchased an item over the Internet. The average American watches over 5 hours of television a day. These are some of the factors that make getting your message to the market a challenge.

Actually, the more you advertise, the less it is heard. Because of the amount of information you see day in and day out. It is like *"trying to fill a teacup with a fire hose."*

The most effective way to get the quality of prospects You need to exponentially grow your business is by REFERRALS.

What about the other three aspects of a successful business? How will this system affect these parts of your business? What about your marketing system? The best approach to marketing your business is to have *"The Right Message Going To The Right Market Using The Right Media."* When you use this referral system you will be accomplishing all three of these goals.

By tapping into your relationships this allows you to focus like a laser on your target markets. I don't think you will find anyone to argue that "word of mouth marketing" is the most effective way to market your business. *"And what better media can you have than someone essentially giving a testimonial about your business while they are helping you schedule an appointment?"*

With this system you will be able to do a lot of things that you can't with a "traditional" direct marketing approach. For example you'll be able to have a successful measuring system for your marketing efforts. You will be able to measure your efforts and results.

CHAPTER 5
IF YOU CAN'T MEASURE IT,
YOU CAN'T MANAGE IT!

Measurement of your activities is one of the critical functions you need to become more successful. With this Referral System, you'll be able to measure the amount of time invested in the process. And you'll be able to know exactly where all of your prospects are coming from. This is a tremendous advantage when building a business.

One big advantage of using this system is in the area of customer service. Many of the approaches used by many organizations are sales oriented approaches. This means the approach is to utilize the "law of averages" system.

The system is as follows: If you make 100 calls and make one sale then you can measure your activity needed to succeed. If it takes 100 calls to make one sale then it takes 200 calls to make two sales and you just measure it right on out to the point if you want to make 10 sales you need to make 1000 calls. This way you can plan your month. You know the number of telephone calls needed to book your appointments, and the number of appointment to make sales, etc. The big problem you have with this approach is that you have no time left to provide any customer service to the people you've sold in the past.

And you know how critical it is to be able to have time to communicate with your customers. It's 5 times easier to sell to a customer you currently have than it is to sell to someone you've never done business with before. But if you don't have time to invest with your current customers it will make it 5 times harder to make another sale.

With this system you will cut your selling time drastically because you get others to help you prospect. *"You are leveraging your relationships and working smarter."*

This system also helps you in the fourth area and that is to be <u>organized more effectively</u>. Again, this system is going to help you **save a tremendous amount of time** for you to use to do other things. You can develop more relationships, spend less time working and invest more time with your family, have more time for your hobbies or lifestyle, or maybe get more involved with your favorite charity. It's your time to do what ever you want to do.

CHAPTER 6
MARKETING EVERY DAY IS KEY TO BUILDING A PROSPEROUS BUSINESS

Have I sold you on the fact that prospecting is the most important step in the sales process? You need to do something everyday to market your business. If you wait for someone else to market your business for you, it'll never happen.

What are the two kinds of ways to approach marketing your business? One way is the direct marketing method. This method approaches prospects directly meaning there is not an introduction to the decision maker by someone having influence with that decision maker.

There is no previous relationship to bridge the gap between the prospect and you. There are many different kinds of direct marketing techniques being used. First, the least effective is "cold calling". You already know about this method. If you want to get a little more effective then you next go to advertising on television, the radio, and the local newspaper, maybe a trade journal.

The challenge with this method is; First, there is not an introduction to the prospect on your behalf. Second, it is very difficult for you to measure the results of your advertising. You usually just don't know where your prospects are coming from. It's tough for you to calculate how much each client is costing for you to generate.

You may want to try the different coupons because they seem so inexpensive. But what is really expensive and inexpensive when it comes to advertising? If you spend $200.00 and don't get a single client, is that a good deal? What if you spend $400.00 and get two new clients, is that a better deal for you? At least you achieved two new clients at a cost of $200.00 each. But unless you are very skilled in these areas your return is very little.

Another way you might try to market you business is the very popular method of "networking". You may have attended networking functions in the past. I have attended several through the years.

You may find the networking functions to be a way to generate "passive referrals". You may be asking, what are "passive referrals?" With the "passive referral" system several things happen. First you may go to a networking meeting and invest a lot of time and money, you eat a lot, and drink a lot, and when it's over you never know if you are going to receive any referrals or not.

If you do receive any referrals you very rarely know the quality of referral until you invest a lot of time with your prospect. You may get a referral but never know where they came from. You generally will never know how many referrals you'll receive on a monthly basis. And you're not properly positioned with an introduction to the referral. These are a few of the characteristics of a passive referral.

What Is The Difference Between A Passive Referral And A Proactive Referral?

But what about a **Proactive Referral System?** What is the difference? A proactive system has many different characteristics. **First,** you know the type of prospect you are getting from the system because you control the process.

Second, you now have your partner searching and targeting the kind of prospect you are seeking.

Third, you know how many prospects you are going to have referred your way because you are controlling the process.

Fourth, you know exactly where your referrals are coming from.

Fifth, you are definitely positioned from a position of

strength with the prospect because of the **introduction** you are receiving from your referral partner.

Another of the popular tactics people like to talk about is called **"lead sharing".** With lead sharing the first person gives the second person a name of a person or company they know about. The conversation would go something like this, *"Bill, I saw a new building going up last week. I bet they will need either your product or service. Here's the address of the location."*

I once knew a VP in a bank that came up with an idea to generate more "referrals" for the bank. She constructed a plan and it went as follows, She said, *"I will give any employee a $5.00 reward for each lead you bring to me within the next 12 months."* So one lady gave her one hundred and five names and telephone numbers. The VP had to cut her a check for $525.00 for the list. How many sales do you think she made from that list? She made zero sales!.

Why didn't she make any sales? She had 105 leads. Guess where the lady who gave her the list, got the leads? You're right. She got them out of the telephone directory.

So when you have a lead you really just have a <u>"cold call"</u> and the reason is because there is **no introduction on your behalf.** There is no **relationship or trust** built into the equation.

Another method of direct marketing is "speeches and seminars".

Most people are under the assumption that if a person is able to get up in front of a crowd and talk they must have something on the ball. So many times you will see people marketing their business using the seminar method.

There are some people who have been successful with this system. But normally most people struggle with this approach. If you've ever put together seminars or speeches you know how expensive and time consuming they are and how much effort these methods take. More often than not this method is a lot of expensive work with very little return on investment.

CHAPTER 7

WHAT ARE THE DISADVANTAGES WITH RUNNING YOUR BUSINESS WITH INCORRECTLY EXECUTED DIRECT MARKETING?

What are some of the disadvantages of running your business with a direct marketing approach such as some of the ones we've listed above?

First, they are very expensive.

Second, your prospects are skeptical of you when they first meet you because there is no relationship prior to your meeting. If there is no relationship to connect you with the prospect, then most people will be price shoppers.

Third, there is usually a sales orientation in the organization. This means there is a focus on sales but very little focus on customer service. Fourth, it is very difficult to determine what's working and what isn't. It's difficult to determine where your prospects are coming from if you aren't getting them to raise their hands and ask for you to come to see them.

Using direct marketing methods, that are **incorrectly done**, to generate more business, is expensive, ineffective and leads to increased stress, turnover, and career burnout.

One of the methods we don't want to forget is, **"BRANDING"**. This is a hot "buzzword" in the advertising community. However, you probably don't have the gigantic budget it takes to brand your company's name. It takes a lot of advertising over a long period of time. **Branding** is good in theory but usually the large companies are the only ones having a big enough budget to do **"BRAND"** advertising.

CHAPTER 8

WHAT ARE THE DIFFERENT SOURCES FOR REFERRALS?

So now that you've heard of some of the things that don't work, you may be asking yourself, "what does work?" The most effective method you can use is a system based on relationships. What do I mean by this? You want to generate your prospects from the relationships you've formed.

Why is the **Relationship** critical? Because the relationship will be a bridge that will connect the **"TRUST GAP"** that stands between you and your prospect. The trust gap is like you being on one side of a canyon and your prospect on the other side. The less the prospect knows about you, the wider the gap.

You won't be able to do capture the prospect as a client until you and the prospect are on the same side of the canyon. When you have a **true referral**, you have instant credibility with the prospect and the gap is instantly closed.

What are some of the sources you have for generating referrals?

There are four different kinds of relationship prospects for you to tap into.

The first one you can use is called a "**Center Of Influence**". A **"Center Of Influence"** is someone who is influential in an industry, community, business, organization, etc. They believe in you and what you do and they are willing to introduce you to qualified prospects. The more influential the person is the easier it will be for you to set appointments when your **"Center Of Influence"** refers you.

Another relationship source is a **"Referral Partner"**. A **"Referral Partner"** is someone you can team up with to refer to. These relationships are easy to arrange because you can refer your partner and your partner can refer you. The reason I say these are easy to arrange is because it is a Win/Win situation. **You get a referral from your partner and your partner gets a referral from you**. This makes it a Win/Win relationship. The system has a built-in-reward for the referrals.

The third source for generating relationship-based referrals are your **"Clients."** Your clients are a virtual gold mine. This is a resource that most people never tap into. You may be asking why I say it is a gold mine that people never tap into?   Here's the answer.

 Remember that in sales one of the key components needed before people will do business with you is **"Trust"**. (People buy from you for three reasons. They like you; They trust you; You have a product or service that people need. **People must trust you** before they will buy from you.)

 Since your clients have bought from you and they continue to buy from you, **then they must trust you**. The trust factor is also important in the referral system. Since your clients already trust you then **they are more or less waiting for you to ask them to refer you**. Believe me, this is a gold mine waiting to be tapped.

Use A "Target List" Used To Generate Referrals?

The last proactive Referral Method is also a relationship-based Referral system. This method is extremely effective but is greatly under used. This source is titled **"Making A List Of Companies To Target For Referrals"**. I have taught this method to hundreds of people who have successfully put it into practice.

It is a very simple process. First list about 20 names of companies or individuals on a sheet of paper. List the company's name or individuals name, the address, and any other contact information you may have available.

When you have meetings with anyone you have a good relationship with, they could be client; referral partners; or centers of influence; a networking group; you take one simple action step. You ask the people if they would be open to reviewing the list you have with you.

You then ask them if they know anyone on the list if they would feel comfortable referring you to that person by introducing you.

(NOTE: Asking for an introduction is less threatening then asking for a Referral.)

This is very effective in helping you generate referrals. The reason it is so effective is it takes all the thinking out of the process for your partner. You have the list and the names. Your partner isn't put in a position to find someone for you. You have the names on the list and your partner either knows them or they don't. You can put together as many lists as you want. I would suggest you have several sheets with about 20 names on them.

You have just learned four different types of ways to generate business. You will find that all four are very effective. **I didn't list them in order of effectiveness.** (They all can be effective if you use them. They aren't very effective if you don't.) You may find that one system may work better for you than the other three. Find the most effective for you and use it.

CHAPTER 9

WHAT ARE THE ADVANTAGES FROM OBTAINING CLIENTS FROM THESE "RELATIONSHIP-BASED METHODS OF PROSPECTING?

The four systems are all relationship based. Therefore you will see certain things happen in your business. **First**, when you are referred to a prospect, trust is built quickly. **Second**, when you meet with the prospect they are more likely to share their needs. **Third,** the prospect already has a great impression of you before you meet. This is accomplished because of the way you were introduced to them. (You can control the introduction. This is key. You can be introduced to a prospect any way you want so you can be positioned from a position of strength in the sales process.)

Fourth, you will produce a customer service orientation within your business and not a sales orientation. This means you are going to have more time to focus on serving your customers and building even a deeper relationship with them.

And **Fifth,** you will have 5 to 10 times less sales activity.

What does this mean for you? This will be a tremendous time-management tool. The reason? You're going to be able to make your sales 5 to 10 times FASTER. What you will find when you implement this system is that **you will** **generate more sales and do it in less time**.

One of the qualities of successful people is the practice of **goal setting.** I am going to help you complete a simple exercise that will help you determine how many referrals you need a month to achieve your goals.

The first part of the formula is this, how many Referrals do you have to get to make a sale? For example if you get 10 referrals how many of those will you sell? Can you sell half of them? If you can, then you have a 50% closing ratio.

The second part of the question is this, when you make a "better than average" sale, what is your commission? Suppose your average commission is $1000.00 per sale and it takes two referrals to make a sale. You then divide $1000.00 by two (for the two referrals it took to make the sale) and you will find that number to be $500.00. So each referral would be worth $500.00 a piece for you.

Now all you have to do is to determine the amount of income you want to have on a monthly basis and divide that number by $500.00. This will give you the number of referrals you need to generate on a monthly basis.

For example if you wanted your income to be $10,000.00 a month then you would need **20 referrals a month**. If you want your income to be $5000.00 a month then you would only need **10 referrals a month**. So you see by using this system you can now become proactive by planning and controlling your sales for the month.

I can assure you that using this system will put extra money in your pocket and will put the fun back in prospecting for you. But it is like a hammer. You can buy a hammer and lay it on top of a table. You can talk to your hammer all day long. But until you pick it up and put it into action, it won't be any benefit to you. This system is the same. **It Won't Work For You Until You Get Into Action.**

Chapter 10

Developing A Description Of The People You Want To Be Referred To.

Creating A Plan With A
Strategy Is Your Key To Succeed

In this session you'll learn how to specifically target the market you want for your business. In the beginning of this book you learned the difference between the rifle approach vs. the shotgun approach. If you want to work smarter, one of the first steps to take is to have a **clear, concise** picture of the prospect you need to build your business. You've probably have heard the quote, *"be careful what you wish for because you might just get it."*

That is especially true with this system. **You usually get what you ask for**. So if your goal is to work smarter then you must have a **clear, concise** picture of the prospects you're seeking. Then you can clearly describe the prospects to your partner. Your may ask, *"why is this important?"*

The answer is: For you to become more successful you must have a specific target to aim for. I would be willing to bet you that you can go to the local retail store and buy a small disposable camera and you can learn to take much better photographs than any of the professionals with their very expensive cameras and lenses.

That is providing you can do one thing that the professional is not allowed to do. What's that? **The ability to FOCUS.** If you are allowed to focus on your subject but the professional isn't then your photographs will be much better time and time again. If you are allowed to focus <u>you will have clear, precise results</u>. The professionals results will be vague, fuzzy, and out of focus. Their result will not be clear.

You Need To Be Focused!

I want to tell you a story about a very successful car salesman. His name is David Thomas. David worked for Sewell Cadillac in Dallas, Texas. (A great book about customer service is, "**The Sewell Way**.") Around the year 2000 he sold over 400 Lexus automobiles. In 2001 he was targeted for 450 cars sold. Why was he so successful? He sells more cars by himself than most Lexus dealerships in the country.

How does he do it? <u>First,</u> **he is very focused** on selling only Lexus automobiles. <u>Second,</u> he is extremely **focused on obtaining Referrals to his target market**. I will include a quote from an article in The Dallas

Morning News. Quote. *"This is how David Thomas became Lexus' top salesman: One day, two or three years ago, he stopped at his dry cleaners and parked between a battered Ford Pinto and an old Dodge pickup. I looked around and thought, 'where's my flock?"* recalled Mr. Thomas. *"These did not look like folks in the market for a Lexus."*

At the time, Mr. Thomas was selling "only" 250 to 300 cars a year-about three times the national average-and wanted to do more. So he began a thorough review of his "network" outside the car dealership. "I looked at my barber, my dentist, my banker, my dry-cleaner, everyone I was spending money with," he said. *"I asked, 'are they going to buy a car from me or send people to me who are going to buy a Lexus?'"*

If the answer was "**NO**," he changed them. *"My new cleaner specializes in fur and leather,"* said Mr. Thomas, who put himself through Texas Tech University selling used cars from a lot opened with a loan from his brother. *"There are Mercedes and BMW's parked in front of the cleaners. They know me there as 'the Lexus guy,' and I don't care if they ever learn my name."*

So you can see that Mr. Thomas is very focused on getting specific. He knows exactly the kind of prospect he is seeking and when you become more focused on your prospects you'll find your business will also grow.

When you're building your business, it is just too difficult to go out every day and try to find a new prospect to sell. (Note: To build a successful, prosperous business, you need to have this approach. You want to make a sale to get a customer. Not find a customer to make a sale. Your goal is then to keep that customer coming back for at least 5 years.)

Most sales people attempt to get new clients by "cold calling". No matter what direct marketing method you employee it is very expensive and difficult to find a new prospect and then sell them on you and your company.

You work extremely hard to find a new customer then it's time to go find another one. When you use this approach you are working by yourself. That is a very difficult way to build a business. If you have ever worked in an environment where all of your clients come from cold calling, you already know how difficult this is.

CHAPTER 11
YOU NEED TO WORK
SMARTER, NOT HARDER!!!

I don't have to explain that to you. I want you to keep in mind that "I*t's 5 times easier to make a sale to someone you are already doing business with than it is to acquire a new customer."* Why is this an important concept? Because, when you begin implementing this referral system you are actually making a sale to someone you already have a relationship with. (Or one of your partners have a relationship with.)

You are only selling them on helping you. **You've already done the hard job of selling them on trusting you.** That was the hard part. You already have them in your database. Now all you have to do is to tap into this resource and you will make you job a lot easier.

"Now to make the process even easier you need to be able to paint a clear, concise, pinpoint, picture of the people you are seeking." (NOTE: One of the major mistakes business people make is not being precise in their target market. This next statement is the "kiss of death" when it comes to getting referrals. Someone asks you, **"Who is your Ideal client?"** And your response is, **"Everyone is my Ideal client because everyone needs**

what I have." WRONG. The more specific you can be the easier it is to get referrals. Remember, people buy what they want, not what they need.) This is essential to help your partners identify prospects for you. They want to help you but you have probably never asked them in the correct way.

How Do You Find People
To Refer To You?

How do you begin the process of defining the specific market you want to target?   Your first activity is to review your client list. The question you may be asking yourself is, **"what/who am I looking for?"** You want to evaluate you client base to find out the type of clients that will help your income grow and to also identify the kinds of clients that are costing you a great deal of time and money.

You may ask the question, **"what are my clients costing me?"** Some of them are costing you your most precious asset, those assets are your time and your energy. You'll probably find that the 80/20 rule will apply to your business. Are you familiar with Pareto's Principle?

Pareto stated that 80% of your activities produce 20% of your results. And that 20% of your activities will produce 80% of your results. You will also find the 80/20 rule will apply to several aspects of your life. You may find it to be very true with your client base.

You will probably find that 20% of your clients will produce 80% of your income or commissions. And the other 80% of your clients will produce the other 20% of your income or commission. What this means for you is that you will probably spend most of your time working with and servicing the 80% of your clients "**who only produce a small amount of your income.**"

They will require more servicing and you will have some who will cost you money. Wouldn't it be important for you to know which group you want to be referred to? So this is a simple exercise for you to complete. This will start you on the path of developing a clear, powerful description of your prospects.

Analyze Your Clients and Then Create A Clear, Concise, Specific Picture For The Kinds Of Prospects
You Want To Be Referred Too!

Your first step is to obtain a complete list of all of your clients you have in your database. You will find that in your database you will have four different types of clients. What you are going to do is to divide your database into four separate categories.

The top category of your clients will be your most profitable. So I want you to identify the **top 10% of your client list**. For example if you have 1000 clients then approximately your top 100 clients are the ones you first want to target.

If you have 100 clients then approximately your top 10 will make up this group. You may have a few more or a few less than the exact number but it will be approximately 10%. You are going to call these top 10% your "platinum" group. Another word you can use for this top 10% could be your **"IDEAL CLIENTS"**.

What you will find is that this group will account for only approximately **10% of you client base but they will produce 50% of your PROFITS OR COMMISSIONS.** This is the first group you are going to develop a description for. I want you to be as specific and detailed as you can when you describe this group.

You will begin by making a rough draft of a description of this group. You will add as many different descriptive adjectives as you can come up with and then you will fine-tune it later.

CHAPTER 12

THE MORE SPECIFIC YOU MAKE YOUR DESCRIPTION OF WHO YOU WANT TO BE REFERRED TO, THE EASIER IT WILL BE FOR PEOPLE TO REFER TO YOU

What are some of the areas you want to focus on when you are putting together a description? One of the first items to focus on with your IDEAL group is to identify your client's position in the company.

Are they the president, owner, or HR person? Do they work in engineering, the IT department, management, or are they the CFO? If they are a professional are they a dentist, doctor, attorney, CPA, business owner, or another type of professional? What if they aren't in business for themselves but work for someone else? You then need to have a description of that individual.

(NOTE: A great example or template for identifying your prospects is to find a copy of the book "**The Purpose Driven Church" by Rick Warren**. You then review chapters 9, 10, and 11. That resource is a great template for you to follow to write a description of the people you want to be referred to.)

To generate the next part of the description, list the type of industry your client belongs too. You may be in an industry where your **IDEAL** client is a banker, an attorney, or a doctor. (Or if they're an individual you might list the organizations they belong to, their hobbies, etc. Basically the demographics for that group.)

Only you can determine your **IDEAL** clients..   If you own an electrical company maybe your **IDEAL** client owns a construction company.

If you are a Realtor maybe your **IDEAL** referral client could be a banker. What you want to identify is where your best accounts are coming from. **When you review the top 10% or your client list you should get a clear picture of the industry that is best for you.**

Are there any other factors that come into play? How about the amount of your client's income? What about the number of years they've been in business? How about the size of the corporation? Is a certain size of business better for you? Your **IDEAL** client could be a corporation with greater than 500 employees. Maybe your best account is a company with 50 employees. You will discover this while you are reviewing you list.

Are there any unique characteristics that are important about your prospect? Maybe your best client is a "not-for-profit" business. Maybe it is a privately held company. Again, put as much information together as possible. So when you have organized the information you may have a description such as the following.

Your **IDEAL** client description may be; *"The president of a fortune 500 company who has been in business at least 10 years and sells electronic equipment to the computer industry. The company must be*

within a 100-mile radius of your office and you must be able to get an appointment with the decision-maker. They also need the product or service you sell and have a history of purchasing value and service and don't necessarily want to be the lowest bidder."

This is just an example of what a description of a **IDEAL** client may look like for you.

So let's have a short review of the first kind of client you are looking for. You will eventually have a description for four different kinds of prospects. But now you are looking for a **IDEAL** prospect. <u>This prospect is similar to the top 10% of the clients you already have.</u>

The great thing about this process is that you can now begin working **"SMARTER"** because you can now identify the number of **IDEAL** accounts you possess. Once you have done that **you can then focus on setting**

goes <u>**to develop more of these accounts**</u> because you now have the method and system to target these kinds of clients.

"Better Than Average Clients Pay Your Bills"

The second kind of client you will create a description for are the clients on your list below your **"<u>IDEAL</u>"** clients. So review your client list and now identify the next 50% to 70 % of clients below your **IDEAL** clients. You will name these clients your **"BETTER-THAN-AVERAGE"** clients. (Or you could call them Bread-And-Butter accounts.)

Your **BETTER-THAN-AVERAGE** clients will account for 50% to 70% of your client volume. But how much of your profit will they account for? This group will generate about 30% of your profit or commissions. So even though they make up a major part of your account base they will only account for about 30% of your income.

These are the accounts that provide the cash flow to keep your business running. They will help you keep the doors open. It is important for you to have an excellent description of these first two kinds of clients because these are the ones you want to be referred to. Your **"BETTER-THAN-AVERAGE"** client description will be a little different than your **IDEAL**.

Your Better-Than-Average clients will not produce as much money for you as your **IDEAL** Clients will.   They may not invest as much money on an annual basis with you. But you need to have a clear description of this group. The best way to do make that description is to review your client list and find the differences between your **IDEAL** accounts and your **BETTER-THAN-AVERAGE** accounts.

You will find some differences, otherwise both would be the same. Again you want to be as specific as possible when describing this group.

So to this point you should have a good, clear, specific description of both your **IDEAL** and **BETTER-THAN-AVERAGE** clients.

Chapter 13

"It's Just As Important To Know Who You Don't Want As It Is To Know Who You Want"

Now you move to the third kind of clients on your list. You will name these clients your **Marginally Profitable (MP) clients.** As you review your client list you will find that about 20% to 40 % of your clients below your Better-Than-Average will be the (MP) clients.

The idea to keep in mind here is that you may not earn much money on these clients. In some cases you may find that you will only break even. When you review your list make sure you don't have an excessive number of (MP) clients on it. (Remember, Pareto's Principle, the 80/20 rule. This group and the next group will be the groups you'll spend most of your time with.)

If you find that you do have a large number of (MP) clients you will also find you will spend a majority of your service time with these clients. It is just as important to know who "you don't want" as it is to know "who you want" as a client.

You will occasionally get referred to the (MP) clients but I would suggest you try to get referred mainly to your

<u>**IDEAL**</u> and "**BETTER-THAN-AVERAGE**" accounts. **This is the smart way to really build your business.** Remember TIME is critical for you when it comes to running and building your business.

(You may even choose to refer the **Marginally Profitable** to your competitors.) <u>If you want to keep them it means that you're hungry for a sale and you can't see that the **marginally profitable clients** are actually using most of your time and keeping you from growing.</u>

What is the major reason this group will keep you from growing? **"Birds of a feather flock together."** Usually, the only people **Marginally Profitable** can refer you to are other **Marginally Profitable** prospects. These are the people they usually associate with.

(PLEASE NOTE: This doesn't mean they are not good people. It just means they may not be a fit for the kind of prospects you're looking for.)

Send Your Undesirable Clients
To Your Competitors!!

The fourth type of account you will have is called an **"Undesirable"** account. Why will you call these your **Undesirable** accounts? They are very heavy to carry and in the long run they aren't worth much to you.   When it comes to servicing an "**Undesirable**" account you'll find that most often you will lose money on these accounts for several reasons. First, the majority of these accounts are small sales but they require a lot of your time because the client is continually complaining.

 Many times they may want a refund or want you to give them something for free. The key to focus on with this group is that they take up a lot of your time and nothing you can do will please them. You may just want to send them to your competitor. Plus the other thing that may happen is that they will stick with you as a client **but they constantly complain** to their friends, relatives, and anyone who will listen about your lousy service or product. They will also tell everyone how **CHEAP** you are because you may have dropped your price to get them as a customer.

You definitely want to be able to identify this group. (I know several business professionals who slow their growth by taking on too many **Marginally Profitable or Undesirable clients.** Why do they do this? They've convinced themselves that they don't take much of their time or their staffs time. But if they were to do a thorough analysis of their client base they would probably find that they were wrong.)

These are ones for sure that you don't want to be referred to. As a matter of fact if someone refers an

Undesirable or **(MP)** account to you I would suggest that you politely thank the person for the referral and request either someone in the **IDEAL or Better-Than-Average** group.

If you thoroughly study you client list you will also find that the clients from the **IDEAL** and **"Better-Than-Average"** section come from relationship based sources. These referrals will come from **clients, centers of influence, or referral partners**.

You will then find that the **(MP)** and "Undesirable" usually come from direct sources. These direct sources are usually advertising sources, that are done incorrectly. Coupons, yellow-page ads, etc. The prospect finds you directly **without an introduction by** someone having influence with the prospect.

Review And Summary

When people are thinking about making a major purchase, they usually ask a friend, neighbor, co-worker, relative, etc. where they bought the product or service. And if that person was happy with their purchase they will then call and likely buy because of the recommendation.

Think about it. If you are going to make a decision to invest a lot of money either on a product or service how do you go about finding someone to provide that product or service?

You usually ask a friend, relative, coworker, etc., if they've ever made a purchase similar to what you are considering. If they have made a similar purchase then you may inquire about who they bought from. If you get a good response or report then you probably will call the person or company you were referred to and inquire. Very seldom will you look for an ad when you are seeking to make a major purchase. (That's not to say that you wouldn't buy a high ticket item from an add if it is a good ad that is properly created. It's just that most ads are a waste of your money because they are constructed incorrectly.)

At this point it is important for you to have a clear description of all four of the clients you want or don't want to do business with. You will even want to write out a description of each one. The reason having a written description is valuable is when you give your description to a referral source they'll have a tendency to keep it. It will then constantly remind them of your request for a referral and the kind of referral you are wanting, each time they look at it.

If you have letterhead for your business it would be smart to write a description of all four on your letterhead. This will give you the **"slight-edge" on obtaining referrals.** You can share the descriptions with your centers of influence, your clients, and your referral partners. Plus you can **leave a copy of your descriptions** behind so they can be reminded of the kinds of prospects you are searching for. You will also look much more professional.

At this point in your system you are working much smarter because you are now using the **rifle approach** to build your business.

Chapter 14
What Are The
Referrability Habits?

(They Seem So Simple Yet
They Are So Very Powerful And Critical.)

One of the questions you may be asking yourself is; **"Why should I focus on building relationships?"** Why would that be more important than placing an ad in the trade journal or on the radio? How about television? How about the Internet? Isn't social media where everyone is going these days? Why shouldn't I just advertise my business instead of going to the trouble of building relationships?

There are many answers to these questions. However, before you learn the answer you must first ask yourself this question. *"How successful do you want to become?"* If you just want a little bit of success, then I suppose to focus on building relationships is not really that important to you? But if you want to be "**mega-successful**" then focusing on building relationships is critical.

Maybe you don't have a huge budget for advertising like

many of the major corporations. Maybe you need to generate results quickly using a modest budget. Maybe you want to use some "Grass-Roots-Guerrilla-Marketing-Strategies. There are many advantages of generating business using the Referral System. <u>Many times you will generate several new clients with virtually no outlay of cash at all.</u>

If you do invest money in the process, often it will be after your prospect has become a client. Plus with most forms of advertising you never really know what's working and what isn't. P.T. Barnum was considered a master at advertising and promotions. He was quoted as saying, ***"I know half of my advertising is working. I just wish I knew which half."*** Often if you invest in a mountain of advertising it may work. You just may not know what's working and what isn't. The beauty of this Referral System is that you **know exactly what is working and what isn't.** <u>You can measure 100% of your efforts.</u>

Most Of Your Rewards And Relationships In Life Comes From Referrals

When you think about most of the advances and growth in your business and personal life you will probably find that the majority of those advances came from some connection with another individual. Most of your friendships or personal relationships have either <u>come from an introduction</u> from someone else or you developed the relationship from one of the organizations you belong to. **Either way those advances were a result of a RELATIONSHIP source.**

So you don't have to be a phi beta kappa from M.I.T to figure out that if you want to become more successful in both personal and business life that the most effective way to do that is to develop your relationship skills? Notice that I said, ***"develop your relationship skills"***.

Building relationships is a skill. It is a skill that you can learn. The skills aren't difficult, but most people won't develop them because it takes effort. The skills aren't reserved for just a few. It just takes a little changing of thinking on your part plus taking the few actions I'm going to suggest. In this section you will learn the "**basic fundamentals**" to develop and build relationships.

CHAPTER 15
WHY AREN'T YOUR RECEIVING MORE REFERRALS?

If you are not receiving referrals, or maybe you are receiving just an occasional referral, then one of three things may be happening. First, you may be positioned to receive referrals but you simply AREN'T ASKING for them. You've probably heard this saying, "*80% of success is just showing up.*" This applies to this system. Often you can generate a large list of referrals just by simply asking.

There may be people all around you who would be eager to help you build your business but you simply aren't asking them. We've discussed earlier some of the reasons you may not be asking for referrals. But I've seen it happen so many times before. Someone like you may belong to many organizations.

They could be professional, civic, or social organizations. And there may be many people willing to help you get an introduction to a new prospect but you just haven't learned the best way to approach (ask) them. It's understandable that you are a little reluctant to ask. **You and I were conditioned for years in our school**

system to answer questions, not ask them.

Wasn't that what you were taught for at least 12 years and many of you even more than that. Day after day the teacher asked you questions and you were to respond with an answer. <u>We just weren't taught the skills and attitudes to ask question</u>s. So isn't it logical that after you graduated from school and now you are responsible for producing results that the last thing you are open to and good at is "A**sking Questions**?"

So now you are out in the work place and you want to generate more business, the last thing you are thinking about doing is asking someone questions. You've investing a lot of time and effort cultivating your relationships either with your clients or friends and you don't want to jeopardize that relationship.

However, once you learn the proper approaches (the right things to say) to asking, the floodgates could open and new business could pour in. **So maybe one of the reasons you aren't getting referral introductions to prospects is just simply that you aren't asking for them.**

What about the second reason you may not be getting referrals. Maybe in the past you have asked for referrals but failed to get anyone interested in helping you. Maybe you received a response like this, *"I would like to help you but I just don't know anyone that might be a good fit for you"*.

Or they may respond, *"I just can't think of anyone right off hand. As soon as I do think of someone I'll give you a call."* Then you wait for them to call <u>but they never do</u>. This could be a simple matter of a few basic fundamentals that you aren't using. In this book you will learn the basic fundamentals so this will never be a problem for you again.

You are going to learn fundamentals that will seem so simple to you that you can't really believe they'll work. You may even say something like, *"that's just plain common sense."* But trust me, they will work. These fundamentals are built around simple but powerful actions. These actions are so simple that anyone can learn them.

You will learn each of the actions to take plus you'll learn the psychology behind each of them. You will learn why they are powerful and after you learn them <u>you can begin implementing them immediately</u>.

CHAPTER 16
THE REFERRABILITY HABITS

These actions <u>are not listed</u> in any order of importance. **They are all important**. You can't just use one and forget the others. You must employ all of them. But don't worry. They are so simple and natural you will be able to put them into practice easily.

Fundamental One:
Always Show Up On Time

The first fundamental revolves around "time". The fundamental rule is, "**<u>Always show up on time</u>**". This seems so simple but it is a powerful fundamental. The reason it is one of the fundamentals is that in our culture "**TIME**" is a big deal. Everyone is trying to manage their "**time.**" Everyone is trying to get more "**time**". People are pressed for "**time.**"

You will find that people have less "**time**" than ever before to do the things they really love to do. (Especially to spend time with their family or on their hobbies.) You will find that people usually get upset if you schedule a meeting with them and show up even 5 minutes late. (They'll say something like, "***that's alright or no problem***") If you apologize for being late the other person will say something to you like, "***it's not a big*** *deal.*"

But in the back of their mind they file it away because what you have just "non-verbally" told this person is the following. *"I know I asked you to scheduled this meeting with me but my time is more important than yours. The reason you know this is that I showed up late and therefore I'm telling you that my time is more important than yours. Now let me sell you something."*

The other person may say it's not a big deal but they will remember it the next time you attempt to schedule a meeting with them. They will definitely remember this if you ask them to refer you.

So one of the fundamentals of your system to gain more referrals is to "**Always be on time.**" Have you heard this saying, "*if you're not early, you're late*". Again the person you call on may tell you that it doesn't matter that you were a little late but when it comes to asking for a referral from that person they subconsciously remember if you have been on time for a meeting or late for that meeting.

Their internal voice is telling them not to refer to you because they don't want to take a chance that you will be late to a meeting to the person they referred you to. (Remember, they may have invested years building a relationship with the person you're wanting referred to.)

That wouldn't look good for the person referring you. Also, they wouldn't want to take a chance that you might be late and waste some of the time of the person they referred to you. That could damage the relationship between the person referring you and their friend or client.

However, I am going to guess that if you are enough of a professional that you're a person who is always on time. So I'm going to guess that this is an action step you are already taking.

Fundamental Two:
"Say Please And Thank You."

The next fundamental is really going to seem common sense to you. You may think that it isn't that important. But let me assure you, it is! We are living in an era where technology is at an all time high. We have never been so swamped in technology. You have computers, cell phones, text messaging, e-mail, the Internet, the list is endless.

The company running my e-mail and web hosting service doesn't want to talk to me on the telephone or in person when I have a problem or a question. They want me to e-mail them. They don't want the personal contact. This is getting more and more commonplace in our culture that people really don't want the personal contact.

What does this mean to you? It means it's getting harder and harder to contact people one-on-one. If you have less and less personal contact that means business is becoming less personal. That's why this fundamental is even more critical.

The second fundamental is to always, **"Say please and thank you."** When you Say "**please and thank you**" you are showing respect for the other person. Again this is a part of our culture that is diminishing. <u>The respect of others isn't as commonplace as it used to be.</u> Our population has doubled over the last 50 years. Cities are getting larger and larger. They are getting less and less personal. We are living in a more impersonal world.

If you want to conduct a small experiment, go to your local mall and hang out for a few hours. When you see someone coming into the mall just open the door for them. See how many are gracious enough to give a gesture of thanks,<u> to say thank you</u>. Some will but many won't, especially the younger crowd. Now you may be asking, what has this to do with my referral system? **Again, this goes back to asking someone to introduce you to one of their best friends or clients**.

You are asking them to work for you. The work you are asking them to do is to target someone who could be a great prospect for you. They have invested years of their time cultivating the relationship. They have qualified this prospect for you, and <u>now you are asking them to introduce the two of you and recommend a meeting</u>.

What is again going through their mind? "***If I introduce my friend or client to this person, will they be treated with respect?***" This message is revolving over and over in their mind like a revolving door at the Hilton. They are thinking that if the person they refer to you isn't treated with respect, again it will look bad for the person referring to you. So can you see the psychology behind saying "**please and thank you**?" It's a small gesture that will set you apart from the crowd.

CHAPTER 17

ALWAYS DO WHAT
YOU SAY YOU'LL DO!

Fundamental Three:
Always do what you say you'll do!

The third fundamental again seems so simple yet it is critical in establishing the habits that will ensure that you will be referred. That is to simply "***always do what you say you will do!***" This again seems so easy but it will give you the **SLIGHT EDGE** when asking to be referred. What is the psychology behind this fundamental? Remember that people will do business with you for three reasons.

First, they must like you. If someone is going to make a buying decision they must like you before they'll buy from you. If they don't like you they won't come out and say they don't like you, <u>they will stall on the decision-making or give you another excuse</u>. **So they must LIKE YOU to buy from you.**

The second factor that must be present before people will do business with you is that you must be able to **bring them a better value or service**. Maybe you can save them money or make them money. Either way there must be some perceived value of doing business with you.

The last reason someone will buy from you is that they must "**TRUST**" you. **Trust** is essential for if they feel you don't have their best interest at heart they won't buy from you. Dale Carnegie said it best when he said, *"people don't care how much you know until they know how much you care?"* I believe that **TRUST is the most critica**l of the three reasons people will buy from you.

An excellent way you develop trust is to "<u>always</u> <u>do what you say you'll do</u>." When you possess this fundamental people will refer to you because they know they can **trust you to take care of the person they are referring.**

Many People Have Betrayed Our Trust

Television is such a big part of most Americans life. It has a tremendous affect on the communicating of daily events that occur in every corner of our country, even the world. What you are exposed to daily are the political officials, corporate officials, religious officials, public officials, the list is endless, of those who have broken their trust with the public.

So as a result of the instant communication capabilities the stories are broken quicker than it takes for your diet drink to lose its fizz. Plus with the advent of 24-hour news channels we are constantly exposed to these stories. **Therefore you may have lost some of the trust in many of the institutions you used to hold sacred.** That's the reason you will find that <u>trust is critical in your success plan</u>.

Anything you can do to increase your trust quotient will be a plus. The best way to do that is to **"always do what you say you'll do".** If you know you can't follow through on a promise, don't make it. Because if you promise to follow through and you don't, it will cause your trust to be diminished with the person you made the promise to.

The interesting thing about this is that <u>people don't care about your excuse even if it is a great one</u>. (In the back of their mind you have now created a little doubt.) Even if your excuse is legitimate.

If something happened that was beyond your control they may forget it but if it wasn't, a little bit of doubt will be placed in their mind. If it happens again then all the doubt will be removed for them. They now believe this is how you operate. <u>The main thing they will remember about you is that you promised to do something then you didn't.</u>

Fundamental Four:
Always Follow Through On Your Promise

The fourth fundamental to concentrate on is another one that seems so simple, yet it is powerful. The fourth fundamental is, "**Always follow through and finish what you start**". Have you ever known anyone that always begins a project only to quit about a third of the way or half of the way through? Then they begin another one. What is the psychology behind this?

Again, if you don't finish what you start you are sending a non-verbal message. The person you are asking for help by referring someone to you may think that if they refer to you then you may provide part of the service and then quit before the service is complete.

They may think, "W*hat if a customer service issue comes up*? *Will this person take care of it or will they take care of part of it and then drop the rest of it*?" They just can't take that chance with one of their friends or clients where **they've invested years** in cultivating relationships.

They may like you, but in the back of their mind there is this nagging doubt that they can't trust that the person they are referring will get the quality of product or service they deserve. So they will stall or put you off when it comes to helping you get referrals.

Build Relationships

Several years ago a client asked me, "How do I go about building relationships?" I asked them, "How do you develop a friendship with someone?"

They said, "I would call them and invite for coffee or lunch. I'd send them a card on a special occasion. I'd find a magazine article about their hobby and send it to them. I'd think of them often and do things for them." I said, There's your answer."

Fundamental Five:
Build Deep, Quality Relationships

Now I will give you the last fundamental. Remember that all of the fundamentals are critical. I have numbered them for you just to point out that there are five fundamentals. There is no order of importance, they are all important. Let me emphasize they are all equally important. The last fundamental is, "**Build quality, deep relationships.**" The relationship will bridge the **TRUST GAP** between you and the prospect they're referring to you.

You can create a list of people you want to develop relationships with. Then on a regular basis (maybe monthly) send them a card, a gift, take them to coffee, take them to lunch, send them an article about their hobby, etc. You can systematically develop relationships with this approach.

This is a great strategy, especially if the people can be a Center Of Influence and refer many Ideal prospects to you.

How many successful hermits have you known? It's very difficult to become successful in life by yourself, no matter how you define success. **Every successful person has had help from someone in their past.** Someone may have introduced them to a mate. They may have been given an introduction to a business partner. Maybe they were introduced to someone they went to work with that launched them into their career path of success.

But think about it. If you had one good solid relationship that helped you succeed wouldn't it be better to have ten-solid-relationships? Or how about having 100-solid-relationships? Would it be easier for you to succeed? I'm going to climb out onto a limb and say that **one of the most important activities you can engage in is to invest time in developing relationships.**

There are hundreds of stories you can find about people who have been deemed successful. You'll find that the majority of these success stories came about because someone they enjoyed a relationship with was instrumental in their achievements.

How Does Attitude Affect Your Outcomes?

What are some of the activities you can engage in that will help you build relationships? The beginning point is your **ATTITUDE about building relationships**. You must believe that an important investment of your time is the time you will invest in cultivating relationships. (What is the reason most people won't do it? Many people haven't sold themselves on the value of it. Therefore, they don't put the effort in it. The rest of the people are just too lazy.)

If you don't truly believe that the time invested building relationships is a good investment then over the long haul you won't continue with the activity.

You must sell yourself that the most critical activity you can be engaged in is the activity of **developing relationships**. This is the first step. The second step is to **have a plan or strategy for developing your relationships**. You must plan to engage in some constant activity to build relationships. You should make this a part of your daily routine just as sales calls are a part of your daily routine. You need to set aside time daily for **"relationship building"** activity. Now your question may be, **"what are some of the activities**?"

Let me give you an example. A firm contacted me about helping to develop their new associates. They had several new associates who had just graduated from college and their specialty schools and were starting in their practice.

The statement the senior partner made to me was this, *"we need you to help our new associates to learn to develop relationships. They are very smart in our profession. They learned everything in school they need to be successful except one thing. They don't know how to develop relationships. They don't even know how to ask someone to go to lunch!"*

I'll give you a list of examples of things you can do to help with relationship building. There is a simple concept to keep in mind here. What would you do to develop a friend? Now think about this. What would you do to develop a friendship with someone? If you are meeting someone for the first time, get as much contact information about them as you can.

Sending Hand-Written Thank-You Notes Will Set You Apart From All Your Competitors

You don't want to come across as a detective working for the police force. But obtain contact information about them. (With the growth of social media you can find massive amounts of information about people on line.)

If it is a business setting, get a business card. After you meet them you can then send a hand written note expressing thanks for the meeting. **(You'll find that one of the best ways to set yourself apart is to send a hand-written Thank-you note.)**

Your hand-written note will have much more meaning than an e-mail because it is more personal. There is also a chance that if you send an e-mail it may not go through the spam filter. Or it could be quickly deleted Or if their e-mail box is like mine I receive between one and two thousand e-mails a week. So it may get lost in the delete series. But you begin the developing the relationship by making contact.

You want to make contact with them at least on a monthly basis.

Now I know what's running through your mind. You're thinking, *"That person is going to think I'm a pest if I keep sending them loads of correspondence."* Or *"Maybe they think I'm stalking them."* I can tell you what people get tired of. They get tired of boring, vanilla information. That's the biggest sin when it comes to developing relationships.

The next step you can consider is to go to lunch with

them or meet for coffee. The more information you can find about them the easier it is to make contact. What do you want to find out about them? (Social media is loaded with information about almost everyone.) There are probably two areas that are most important to the other person. **Their business and their   personal lives. (Their family and hobbies.)**

You want to find out as much as you can about their business. How long have they been there? If they are a business owner, did they start the business from scratch or did they buy it? What sort of products or services do they provide? What are their greatest challenges with running their business? What is their marketplace?

The more you find out about their business the easier it is to find reasons to contact them. Maybe you can find an article in a journal or paper that relates to their industry. You can cut it out and send it to them. <u>If you find an article that has been written about their company, products, services, or accomplishments, cut it out, laminate it, and send it to them. This will definitely make points with them.</u>

What about their personal aspect of their life? Find out about their hobbies, their birthday, and their family members. If they are married do they have any children? If so how old are they? Do they have boys or girls? What are their names?

What's their spouse's name? Are they native to the area? Did they move from another location?   What are their favorite foods? Where do their children go to school? Do they enjoy sports? The list is endless about information that can be gathered. And with the technology available today it is much easier to keep all of that information in a file.

You can now purchase software programs that will organize the data and even notify you when you need to make contact with them. <u>With all the information you've gathered you have only your imagination to limit you from building relationships</u>.

Are you getting the picture? You can organize your information so that you are doing something each week to continually develop relationships. **The time spent doing this will pay off tremendous dividends. <u>(Remember, in building your business, the easiest sale you'll ever make is to a current customer. The second easiest sale to make is to a REFERRAL.)</u>** You may be saying to yourself, *"this sounds like a lot of work to me. I don't have time to do the work I'm supposed to get done as it is."*

"Now you're asking me to build a database and gather all this information and have all these meetings. I just

don't have time." I'm not asking you to do that at all. I'm asking you to begin the process if you aren't already doing this. You incorporate a little each week. **How much time does it take to write a note, or send an e-mail message, or send a clipping of an article?**

If you aren't already involved in the relationship process, target two or three people to begin. As you begin seeing the rewards from increasing your relationships you may see the value of increasing the amount of time you invest in this activity. Let me emphasize to you that one of the fundamentals to working **"smarter-not-harder"** is to have people **help you** build your business.

What better way is there to build your business than to have others helping by searching in their circle of contacts and qualifying and targeting prospects and then making introductions for you.

Chances are you have several people you have excellent relationships with you just haven't had the proper approach to use up to this point.

If you want additional help in this area a good resource is a book by Dale Carnegie. The title is, *"How To Win Friends and Influence People"*. It was written almost 100 years ago but it is definitely still a good resource. Another excellent resource is, *"How To Swim With The Sharks Without Being Eaten Alive,"* by Harvey McKay.

In the following chapters you're going to learn how to put all of this together. You'll learn the **7-step process** that will position you from a **position of strength** each step of the way in the referral process.

CHAPTER 18

THE 7-STEP APPROACH PROCESS TO ALWAYS POSITION YOURSELF FROM A POSITION OF STRENGTH IN THE SALES PROCESS!

This is the section you've been waiting for. In this section you'll learn the communication skills that will "**Sky-Rocket**" your business. Communication is critical to your success. Developing the art of asking questions is a critical skill to have to gather more business.

Have you heard the old saying, "I*t's not what you say, but how you say it, that will determine your results?*"

I want to tell you a story to illustrate the point. There were two priests and each asks essentially the same question to get permission to do something. One is granted his wish the other flatly denied. I'll tell you the story.

The first priest asks his superior, "**Superior, I have a question for you.**" The superior replied, "**Yes, my son, what is your question?**" My question is, " **Do you mind if I smoke while I pray**?" The priest was astonished and replied, *"Heavens no, you may not! You know it is strictly forbidden to smoke in our sanctuary."* He was flatly denied.

The second priest asked his superior, "*Superior, may I ask you a question?*" "*Sure my son,*" was the reply." His question was as follows, "**Do you mind *if I pray* while I smoke**?" The superiors response was, "**Of course you can my son, you know you can pray any time you choose**". He was granted permission.

He asked almost the same question as the first priest but he was granted permission while the first priest was denied. What's the moral to this short story? "***It's not what you say,* but how you say it*, that many times determine how successful you are with your communication skills***". One major key in selling and communication is to develop the Art Of Asking Questions.

You're going to learn the most effective method to approach your sources to generate more business. Many of you may be thinking that you have to be an expert at asking questions or that you have to get a college degree in communication to be successful at this.

Nothing could be farther from the truth. You will learn these skills and if you can **"walk and chew gum at the same time"** you can be successful with this system. This system is easy to learn. Earlier you heard me say that you needed to possess the skill of asking questions.

This is true, however you don't have to have an MBA in communications from Harvard to make this system work. As a matter of fact **I am going to tell you exactly what to say during each step**.

The first step of this system is called the "**Approach**". The approach is just that. What you are going to do is to APPROACH someone you have a relationship with, and this part is very important so pay attention.

The Referral System Is Easier Than You Think. The Only Thing Keeping You From Making It Work, IS YOU!

You are going to approach someone you have a relationship with and you are going to ask them for help. You notice I didn't say you were going to approach a stranger or someone you hardly knew. I said you were going to approach someone you already have a relationship with.

Most of you may be thinking something along this line, *"I don't want to be a bother to them."* Or *"they may think my business is really in trouble if I'm asking for help."* Or you may be thinking, *"I may jeopardize our relationship if I ask for help"*. Again, nothing could be farther from the truth. It has been proven time and time again that your personal and business relationships are eager to help you.

You can read all the sales books in the market place and the ones who know what they are talking about will tell you that **sales is all about positioning yourself with your prospect.** That is precisely what you are going to do in this process. <u>You are positioning yourself with your contact.</u>

The positioning occurs in the first step, the **APPROACH**. As a matter of fact <u>with this system you will be positioning yourself throughout the entire process</u>. What you will have at the end of the process is a <u>qualified prospect</u> and you will be positioned with them in a position of **STRENGTH** and more likely to make a sale.

Remember, the real key here is to be asking people you have a great relationship with for help. You don't want to ask a stranger or someone you barely know.

CHAPTER 19
STEP ONE OF THE 7-STEP PROCESS

Step one: So you may be asking, "*What is the approach?*" The approach is the beginning of the process. The approach will be different for the four different types of referral sources you are approaching. The approach for your "**Center Of Influence**" and your "**Client**" are almost identical. You want to approach both of these from the standpoint of asking for their help.

One of the keys to asking questions is to begin by simply asking your partner if you can ask a question. You begin this process by having a "low-keyed and non-threatening" tone with your question.

This is how it will sound. (Oh, by the way I will pick out randomly the name Bill and use it for all of your examples.) So you begin this way. Remember to be "low-key and non-threatening, "*Bill, do you mind if I ask you a question*?" You will find that 99.99% of the time everyone will reply, "*no, I don't mind at all, what's your question?*" You then proceed.   The first question you ask is, "*Bill, I need your help. Our Business is expanding and I have room for a couple more clients. Would you be willing to introduce me to some people you know who may be a good fit for our business?"* If you have a good relationship with Bill 95% to 99% of the time the response you receive will be, "S*ure, what can I do to help*"?

Or another way for you to ask the question is this, "*Bill, I need your help. Our business is growing and I have room for a few more clients. Would you be willing to introduce me to someone like yourself?*" Again if you have a good relationship with Bill he is going to reply "**yes**," almost 100% of the time.

Your First Question Let's People Know You're Successful, That You're Not Hurting For Business.

Now what have you done with this request? You have positioned yourself because what you are telling Bill with your question is that you are successful because your business is expanding and growing. (This takes care of the fear many business people have of looking like they're begging for business. Or that their business is in trouble.)

So with your first question you are removing the idea that you are begging for business because **you've just told Bill that your business is successful, because it is expanding.**

You will find that there is usually a common response to your question and the response is most often, "**Sure, what do I need to do**"?

(NOTE:. If by the remote, outside chance that your contact would say something along the line of, "**No, I don't believe in helping people**", you politely thank them for their time and move to someone who is more cooperative. This is a **very rare occasion** but eventually you may find it to occur.)

Step Two Is To Schedule A Meeting

When your partner replies, "**Sure, what do I need to do?**" you suggest that you two schedule a meeting to discuss the process. There are several items you need to be aware of here. First, you can schedule to meet anywhere. **But remember you're working smarter to become more successful.** You may want to go to lunch to discuss the idea. However, remember at a restaurant you will have several interruptions.

The waiter or waitress may be coming by often and will interrupt your conversation. Also, there will be other distractions, sounds, people coming and going, and the general atmosphere of a restaurant is one of interruptions. So if your goal is to just talk about the process in an "ice -breaking-manner" then the cafe may work for you.

When you really get serious about the process though, you need to meet in their office or somewhere that's quiet. This has several advantages for you. **First**, you can control the interruptions. When you schedule the meeting you can again position yourself from a position of strength.

When you schedule the meeting you can suggest something along this line. *"Bill, I know you are extremely busy and your time is valuable. I'm like you in that I'm also busy. If we can meet without interruptions, our meeting will go twice as fast."*

Your Center Of Influence Or Client Will See You As Serious About The Process And See You As A professional!

But the major benefit for meeting in their office is that your partner most likely will have all of their contact information filed there. They will have the names of business or social acquaintances. They'll have the lists of organizations they belong to. Also, you need to get as much contact information as you possibly can.

You need the contacts telephone number. Their business number as well as cell phone if possible. You need their company name and address, if pertinent. Also any information about their business or business history you can obtain. You need their e-mail address.

(You will be surprised how many people you can get in touch with quickly by e-mail or Text-messaging that you cannot get in touch with on the telephone).

You also need their web address to again obtain as much information about the company before you meet them. Your partner will have all of this information at their office so the meeting place of choice is the office. If you can't meet at their office then do the best you can with another place. The main objective is to have the meeting and get referrals.

The third benefit of scheduling a meeting to discuss getting introductions is that you are sending another non-verbal message. **You are sending the message that you are a professional and that you are serious about this process**. This will tell your partner that you are very serious about this process and they can trust you with the prospects they are going to introduce to you.

This approach also tells your partner that time is critical to you. You are again telling them in a non-verbal message that you are not going to waste your time, your partner's time, or the time of the person you are being referred to. Can you see how this is again **positioning you with a position of strength?**

Also if you ask them for a certain allotment of time, don't stay past that allotted amount of time unless they ask you to stay. For example if they ask you how much time you will need and you reply, *"**If we don't have any interruptions we won't need more than 30 minutes for our meeting**."*

When your 30 minutes is up, tell them you will leave unless they want you to stay longer. You would handle this in this fashion. *"**Bill, when we scheduled this meeting I told you we would need about 30 minutes. I see that our 30 minutes is up. Do you have a few more minutes or do you have another meeting scheduled**?"*

(When you adhere to these steps of this system your credibility will go even higher with your partner.)

Chapter 20

Developing A Referral Partner

The approach for a "Referral Partner" is a little different than the approach for a "Center Of Influence" or a "Client." For a "Referral Partner" your approach is as follows. *"Bill, would you be open to getting together to discuss ways we might be able to refer business to each other.*

I think that we can help each other market the others business much stronger than we can market our own. Would you be open to meeting with me to explain your business to me and then I can explain more about my business to you. If we develop a win/win relationship then we can help market our businesses for each other.

A win/win relationship would be that I give you a referral and introduction and that you give me a referral and an introduction."

Or another approach can be. *"Bill, what do you think about us meeting and discussing ways we might help each other market our businesses. Tell me who you're looking for and I'll tell you who I'm looking for. We can then search our files and find a match for each other. Are you willing to give it a try?"*

Another approach for your referral partner is as follows. *"Bill, I believe you can help market my business for me and I can help you market your business for you. I believe we can do that much more effectively than we can market for ourselves. Would you be willing to meet and explore ways we may help each other build our businesses".*

One technique you will have a lot of success with is asking a potential referral partner to schedule a time for you to come by to learn more about their company. Your goal is to ask them about their business and find out from your potential referral partner the kinds of clients they are looking for.

If You Approach Your Partner From The Standpoint That You Want To Help Them, They Will Be Much More Receptive To Meeting.

This is how your approach will sound. *"Bill, I would like to schedule some time to come by and learn more about your company. I am heavily involved in the community and I may be able to refer some business to you. Would you be open to this idea?"*

What you will find is that you can schedule a very high percentage of the calls you make using this approach. (The reason? You are putting the focus of your energy on the other person instead of yourself.) Also, when

<u>you go to your meeting, you must stick to the reason
you told the business owner you were coming by.</u>

You don't want to schedule an appointment to go their
company to learn more about what they do and then
when you show up you begin giving a "<u>full-blown</u>" sales
presentation. You must stick to the reason you asked
them to let you come by. If you don't adhere to your
request in your original call the following will happen.
The other person will be put out with you and may ask
you to leave. They sure won't want to continue any
conversation.

What you do want to do is to go to the meeting and
inquire about the owner, the company, their products,
their services, and the kind of clients they are seeking.
In most instances they will stop you after about 30
minutes and ask about you and your company.

You will hear them say something to this effect, "Tell me
about you and your company. Tell me about yourself.
What do you do? What kind of clients are you looking
for? How can I help you?"

This is an excellent approach. But remember you asked
the other person if you could come by. If they don't
inquire about your business, or service, or you, and all
they do is talk about themselves, they probably won't be
a good candidate for a Referral Partner or Center of

Influence.

I would just listen and gather information and if they are the kind of person you feel would make a good referral source or a prospect, follow up with a thank-you note and put them in your sales and marketing funnel.

CHAPTER 21
USING A TARGET LIST
TO GENERATE REFERRALS

Another very useful technique to obtain referrals is the method of "using a list of targeted companies or individuals" to get referrals. Here's how it works. You put together a list of about 20 companies, or individuals, on a single sheet of paper.

You include all the information you have about the company. The name of the contact person you are interested in meeting, the companies name, address, telephone number, etc. As you meet with clients, acquaintances, or referral sources, here's the way you use this strategy.

You give them a copy of your list of companies. You then ask this question, *"Would you mind reviewing this list of companies (or individuals) to see if there is anyone on the list you recognize? If you know someone, would you feel comfortable introducing me to them*?" You can also use this technique to obtain introductions to individuals. This is a very good way to get introductions into companies you have been approaching for an appointment. I used this techniques one time with one of my referral partners and he introduced me to a decision-maker in a trucking company.

I had attempted at least one time a quarter for four years to get an appointment with the owner of the company. My referral partner made <u>one telephone call and introduced me</u> not to the owner but a decision-maker in a certain department.

That decision-maker wanted a referral program developed for their truckers. I was given an introduction, I made one telephone call and obtained an appointment. **I made two presentations and after the second presentation I signed a contract for $30,000.00.**

I would encourage you to use any of these approaches. They will work for you. It will just take you a little time and practice. If you follow the system step-by-step, the way it is designed for you, you can generate business and sales.

So **Step One** for you is the approach. Ask someone to meet with you. **Step Two** is then to schedule the meeting. Again this is helping you to work smarter. <u>You can schedule the meeting to fit into your schedule.</u> You are gaining more control of your time and energy. Once you've scheduled the meeting, you then move to step three.

Step Three Of The 7-Step Referral Process: Describe The Kinds Of Prospects You're Seeking.

In **Step Three** you describe the kind of prospects you want to be introduced to. This is an important step because "**you usually get what you ask for.**" (Note: you developed descriptions in Chapter 12 and this is where you put them to use). What I will suggest for you in this section is to have a clear understanding of a description of the prospect you're seeking.

There are a couple of ways you can do this. One is to have a clear description memorized in your mind.   This will take a little practice to develop a description of your four kinds of clients. The second way is the one I've found most effective.

People Have A Habit Of Keeping Paper To Read

Use a sheet of your letterhead and type a description of each of your four types of clients on this sheet of paper. There are several reasons this is beneficial for you.

First you are not going to have the stress of trying to remember an exact description of each type of prospect.

Second, you will appear more professional.

Third, it will be easier for your source to visualize a good fit for you because you're getting them to use more of their senses in the process. The more you can get your prospect involved with you and your referral process the more successful you will be.

Have you ever heard the saying attributed to Confucius? He said, *"I hear I forget, I see I remember, I do and I learn"*. The more involved with the process you can get your source, the more successful you will become.

The **fourth** benefit of having your description on your letterhead is that when you leave your sources office, you can leave it behind for them to keep. This will be a constant reminder of the kind of referrals you are seeking. This is another way to keep your name in front of others for generating more referrals.

CHAPTER 22

YOU CAN GET REFERRALS
BY TEACHING OTHERS

The **fifth** benefit is for the person you are working with. By taking them through the referral process, you are providing them with valuable knowledge and skills. **By your actions, you are teaching them the Referral System.** You are "**Modeling**" to them the correct method to generate referrals. If they are in a position where referrals are valuable to them <u>you are indirectly teaching them a</u> **valuable marketing skill.**

This brings up an interesting point for you. An excellent method for getting started in the referral process is as follows. You approach someone who is in a position of needing more business and could use referrals. As a matter of fact they would welcome referrals.

Now this is how you approach them. ***"Bill, are referrals important for your business?"*** If they reply "yes." Your next question is: ***Would you like to know a secret of how to get more referrals for you and your business?"***

And most likely Bill would answer, "**Sure, I would love to know how to generate more referrals.**" You then say, "**Let me come by and I will walk you through the Seven**

Step Process for you to learn how to get more and better business using referrals."

You then schedule a meeting with them and take them through the **Seven-Step-Process**, step by step. This is a win-win scenario because your partner learns the steps to get referrals and as a by-product from teaching them the system and following the system step-by-step, **you get referrals and introductions to qualified, targeted prospects.**"

Step Four Of The 7-Step Process

Now let's move to **Step-Four**. In step four you want your resource to search their files or database for prospects for you. They are specifically searching for the kinds of prospects you've described. As they identify prospects for you, you want to take notes as they give you information.

The information you're seeking is contact information. You want the contacts **names, with correct spelling.** I can't emphasize this enough. It is very embarrassing and unprofessional to call on someone and pronounce their incorrectly. Or if you send them a note or card and misspell their name. A persons name is one of their most cherished possessions. If it is misspelled or mispronounced it has a negative impact on that person.

You also want other contact information. **Their company name, telephone number, address, e-mail address, web address, etc.** Also any personal information your resource is willing to share with you. How does the resource know the person they are referring to you? Do they socialize together, are they in clubs together, do they play any sport together, etc.

What you want with this information is to get an idea of the **INFLUENCE** your referral source has with the prospect. The better they know each other the better you will be positioned when you seek to get an introduction.

As your source continues to give you names, make a list of each name with all the information. When your source has finished giving the names and information, make a copy of the list and give it to your Referral source. You now move to the next step.

Step Five Of The 7-Step Process
In step five you will review the list with your resource.

You are reviewing the list to find out how much **influence** your resource has with the prospects they've identified for you.

This is very easy for you to accomplish. All you have to

do is to begin with the first person on the list. You then ask a very simple question about the relationship of the two people.

This is the question you ask. *"Bill, let's review the list. Tell me about the first person you've listed. What I'd like for you to do is to tell me, on a scale of "one-to-ten" with ten being that you are best friends and one means you hardly know them at all, where is your friendship meter on that scale?"*

When you ask this question about the first person on the list your source will give you a number between one and ten. **Now this is very important, because psychologically, if they feel they know the person very well they will give you a number like 7 or 8 or 9 or 10.** If they don't feel they know them very well you will receive a number of 5 or less.

This is a critical step because what you're seeking is a prospect you can receive an excellent introduction to. If the person referring to you doesn't know the prospect very well, **you will not get a good introduction.** Remember you want to work **SMARTER**. You want to maximize your effectiveness. An excellent introduction to the prospect is going to position you with a position of strength in the sales process.

If you receive a number on the scale of 6 or higher you

move to the introduction step with this person.

You proceed through your list and qualify each person using the **"One-To-Ten Method."** What you will now have is a list of prospects with all of them being qualified. The ones who are qualified 6 or higher, you want an introduction to.

The ones qualified 5 or lower you want to put aside and wait until your referral source gets to know them better. (Or if you want to contact this group understand they won't be as good as the others, However, they'll be much better than cold-calls.)

Can you see how you're now working smarter and being more focused on building your business? Now that you have completed this step you are ready for the **Introduction Step.**

CHAPTER 23

INTRODUCTIONS ARE CRITICAL
Step 6 Of the 7-Step Referral Process

<u>Step 6 is the Introduction Step</u>.

Each of the steps in the **7-STEP PROCESS** are critical. So you must pay attention to each step.   This is the step you are going to use to position yourself with the prospect. In this step you will do several things. **<u>First</u>**, you must ask your resource if they are willing to introduce you to the person they have identified.

Most of the time they'll agree. <u>So you have three tasks in this step</u>. First is to find out the communication method they are going to use to introduce you. There are many different methods to use for introductions. One way obviously is for them to introduce you to the prospect with a one-on-one meeting, in person.

Another way to make an introduction is for them to make a telephone call on your behalf. Other methods you will find that work are:

A. For them to write a letter of introduction on your behalf. Your source would write a letter to the person on your list. In the letter they would introduce you and explain why they are writing the letter. They would also include why the prospect should meet with you.

Another way is to have your resource record an introduction on an audio or video recording to take to your prospect. In the recording they will explain why you are being recommended and why you two should meet.

Also, having them make a telephone call to introduce you or schedule a meeting with the three of you. These last two methods are extremely powerful. The reason they are more powerful than the others is because of **the effort required to make the introduction**.

It shows the importance the person Referring places on getting you two together. These are very doable and take a little more time but they can exponentially jump your success rates in sales. The major reason they are so powerful is that they will position you in a position of strength in the sales process.

All of these introductions work because of the concept of someone taking time out of their day to introduce you to someone they know.

So the first part of the introduction step is to determine what method your resource is going to use to introduce you to their contact. The second part of the introduction step is to find out what they are going to say about you. (Remember, the introduction positions you in the sales process with a position of strength.)

You want them to have an introduction that is structured so the prospect is motivated to see you and open to visiting with you about your product or service because of the influence the person referring you has with the prospect.

The first step in this process is to ask your resource what they will say about you when they introduce you. If they don't have a good introduction constructed, then you can help them by coaching them with what to say about you. (**A good strategy here is to have an introduction written out as a script they can go by**.)

(NOTE: *You don't want your partner or client making a sales presentation for you. No one can sell your product or service as good as you. You only want them to give the prospect enough information to schedule an appointment. If they give to much information the prospect may make a prejudgment about what you offer and not want to meet with you.)*

When the introduction is made you want them to talk about the quality of service or product you produce. You want them to talk about the reason they suggest you or your company. You want them to praise your follow up or attention to detail. They may mention the excellent customer service you provide. **You begin positioning yourself** with the prospect with the introduction.

The third part of the introduction step is to get an agreement for the time frame for your introduction to be completed. (This is also a critical part of the introduction process.)

 The faster you can get them to introduce you to your prospect the more success you will enjoy. Your goal is to get an introduction within 48 hours of the meeting with your partner. There is a lot of enthusiasm and energy on the part of your partner. If you can get the introduction completed within a week, that will also work.

 But if you wait for a month or more for the introductions, your chances of getting a new client will go down. The energy and enthusiasm is greatly diminished. So the quicker you can get the introduction the more effective your process will be.

CHAPTER 24

FOLLOW-UP IS KEY

Step Seven In the 7-Step Referral Process

Step number 7 is the follow-up and Reward. This step is not more important than the others however you can invest a lot of effort in this process and if you don't do a good job on this step your work can all go down the drain.

This step also includes the **"REWARD"** section and you will also learn the importance of "scheduling the appointment." You may be asking, "**What is the follow-up step**"? Here's the answer. The follow-up is the part or the system where you position yourself to keep the process moving.

As you are aware, everyone is extremely busy. Several years ago experts were telling us that there was going to be a problem in the United States work environment. The problem was being caused by the popularity of the personal computer and the computer in the office place.

They were telling us that the problem was going to be that you would have a lot of time on your hands as a result of the computer. They were telling us that you were only going to be working 30 hours a week. That you would have so much time on your hands that it was going to be a problem. Let me ask you. *"Have you seen that as a problem?"*

You probably haven't. As a matter of fact, it's just the reverse. We have less time available because you are working more and more hours every week. So your partner or client is taking time out of their day and schedule to help you get referrals. They still have a business or life to run and their day-to-day operations may be very busy.

They will have great intentions to help you but they may have a crisis occur. They may attempt to reach your prospect on your behalf to introduce you. Something may happen on the prospects end that will postpone the process. So to make the best of all your efforts, complete your system with the "**follow-up**" step.

The follow-up is broken down in the following parts.

Part 1. Your partner agrees to make the introduction for you.

Part 2. You will then find out the method they will use and the time frame they allot for the introduction.

Part 3. You ask your partner how you will know if they were successful making contact with your prospect.

Part 4. They will give you a response similar to, *"I will call you and let you know"*. You then thank them for their effort. It would sound something like this.

"Bill, I really appreciate all of your effort in helping me. However, I know how busy you are and I would suspect the person you are referring me to is busy also. You mentioned you were going to call on Tuesday of next week. If I don't hear from you by Wednesday afternoon do you mind if I call to find out where you are in the process?"

If you are sincere and nurturing when you ask this question, the response you will receive will be, *"I don't mind at all. If you don't hear from me feel free to call."*

This approach to the follow-up does several different things to position you from a position of strength. Again it shows that you are a professional because you respect their time. Second, it reassures them that you are sincere about the referral process and that you again show you are a professional because of your detail to follow-up.

They also get the message that if they do refer someone to you, then you will follow-up quickly with the prospect they referred. The other thing this does for you is to take away the anxiety of wondering whether to call your source or wait for them to call you.

You have a plan and a schedule. There is nothing worse than to **feel like a pest** by continuing to call your resource and "**bug**" them about making an introduction.

Now what do you do if your partner agrees to contact the prospect and you're past the allotted time agreed upon for the introduction? You now call them and they tell you they were unable to contact the prospect because the prospect was tied up or out of town.

You then go back through the original steps and begin the process over. Find out the time frame you source is going to make the contact for you and follow up.

Now you are at the point where your source has made the introduction for you. You partner tells you they have introduced you to all the referrals and you can now contact them. Now that the introductions have been made you call the prospect and schedule the appointment. You now have the meetings scheduled and **the rest is up to you to now sell them.**

CHAPTER 25

REWARDING IS CRITICAL

What is the final step of the system for the person who referred you? Your next step is to **reward your partner. This is a critical step in the process.** Many people choose to "reward someone for a referral if the referral turns into business."

Remember, "reward the behavior you want." How do you motivate people to refer to you more? Make the reward exciting, enthusiastic, and fun. If people are excited about the reward they're going to receive they're more likely to refer to you.

At least send a thank you card or call them and personally thank them for their referral.

Rewarding Rules

Rule 1. The larger the account you get from the referral the larger the reward could be.

Rule 2. No matter what happens as a result of your meeting with the prospect, <u>you always reward your source.</u> (You may get a new client or you may not get a client, but you will get a new name to add to your database.) Also, the more fun and enthusiastic you can make referring to you, the more referrals you'll receive.

(NOTE: One of the reasons people don't get more referrals is there is no excitement or enthusiasm for the person referring. I have people tell me all the time that if the Referral turns into a client they will then give a gift. Talk about a way to stifle the Referral Process.)

What are some of the "gifts" you can use to reward your source? You can reward them with a telephone call expressing thanks. You can send a hand written card expressing thanks. Some of the gifts I have used are: gift certificates, lottery tickets, tickets to movies, theater tickets, gift baskets, high-dollar sports gifts. Women love bath and body products.

You can afford to spend several hundred dollars on gifts for referrals when the referral results in an account of several thousand dollars. Use your imagination to give unusual gifts. The point for you is that it is critical to reward everyone who refers to you.

If you have someone going out of their way to help you acquire a new client or contact and they never hear from you again, you'll probably never receive a referral from them ever again.

One question you may have is, *"Should I pay money for referrals*?" I would suggest against that. Here's the reason. If you offer money for referrals people will view their relationship with you as a *"paid sales account executive"*. (NOTE: Also, if you give money, when it is spent it is gone. If you give a gift, every time your Referral source sees it, they think of you. If it's a great gift, they'll think of you in a positive light.)

You will find that the approach of giving cash very rarely works on a long-term basis. Remember, more people are "recognition motivated" than "money motivated."

You should always place a telephone call and express appreciation to go along with the gift you send.

This next statement is very important. **When you gain a new client by a referral, you will find that the new client you have gained will be open to referring to you because the referral process is the method you used for an introduction to them**.

Educate your new client that you obtained them as a client from a referral. And that you expect all your clients to refer to you. Start them off on the right foot about referring. Explain to them the best way to refer to you. Remember, people will usually do what you expect them to do.

You now have the SYSTEM that was previously known to only the top 1% of sales producers   You now have the system to build your business as large as you want. You have a system that you can use to plan with. You can set down at the beginning of the month and plan meetings and actions that will move you towards more referrals.

Your imagination and effort are your only limiting factors now when it comes to growing your business. I wish you all, the best of success and I hope you greatly multiply your income.

Printed in Great Britain
by Amazon